100 Q
500 Nations:
A Guide to
Native America

The Native American
Journalists Association
with
Michigan State University

Read The Spirit Books
an imprint of
David Crumm Media, LLC
Canton, Michigan

For more information and further discussion, visit

news.jrn.msu.edu/culturalcompetence

Cover art and design by
Rick Nease
www.RickNeaseArt.com

Published by
Read The Spirit Books
an imprint of
David Crumm Media, LLC
42015 Ford Rd., Suite 234
Canton, Michigan, USA

For information about customized editions, bulk purchases or permissions, contact David Crumm Media, LLC at info@DavidCrummMedia.com

Contents

Foreword

Welcome and thank you for opening this guide from the Native American Journalists Association. Founded in 1983, NAJA's primary goal is "to improve communications among Native people and between Native Americans and the general public."

With that in mind, NAJA published "100 Questions, 500 Nations: A Guide to Native America" in 1998, the association's 15th year.

In its 30th year, NAJA worked with the Michigan State University School of Journalism to create a new edition of that guide. It is published here as part of the school's series of guides to cultural competence.

This guide and others in the series are intended as first steps. They use journalism to answer questions with accurate, authoritative information. We encourage you to read these answers and to keep asking questions. People experience life in different ways, so they might answer differently. We recommend you talk to many along your journey to understanding.

Thank you.

About this Guide

This is part of a series of guides to cultural competence. They are designed to use journalistic tools to increase understanding. The series is published by the Michigan State University School of Journalism.

This guide about American Indians is the Native American Journalists Association's update of a guide it first published in 1998. That original helped inspire this series of 100-question guides. The series follows a four-dimensional ethic of respect, accuracy, authority and accessibility.

This guide was updated for 2014 by:

* Mary Hudetz (Crow), president of the Native American Journalists Association and editor of Native Peoples Magazine

* Tristan Ahtone (Kiowa of Oklahoma), NAJA treasurer and journalism ethics and initiatives committee chair and New Mexico public health reporter at KUNM.

* Dalton Walker (Ojibwe), NAJA board member and web editor/social media manager at www.gazette.com

* Joe Grimm, editor for the MSU School of Journalism's series of guides to cultural competence

* Thank you to NAJA Executive Director Pamala Silas (Menominee/Oneida)

The original guide was created and developed by Reginald Stuart, corporate recruiter. It was researched and written by Linda Fullerton, St. Paul Pioneer Press. Questions and answers were prepared with the assistance of Elizabeth Homer (Osage of Oklahoma), director of the Office of American Indian Trust; Eric B. Wilson (Nez Perce of Idaho), program analyst, Office of American Indian Trust; Thomas Sweeney (Citizen Potawatomi of Oklahoma), public affairs chief, Bureau of Indian Affairs; Iris Friday (Tlingit of Alaska), publications editor and development director. Assistance came from the National Congress of American Indians, National Indian Gaming Association, American Indian Higher Education Consortium; Labriola National American Indian Data Center and the American Indian Movement. The Wichita Eagle printed it.

— Joe Grimm, series editor
Michigan State University School of Journalism

General

1 Who is an American Indian?

There are millions of people who identify as American Indian or who have Indian ancestry. That does not make them all American Indians in the eyes of tribes or the federal government. The federal government considers someone American Indian if he or she belongs to a federally recognized tribe. Individual tribes have the exclusive right to determine their own membership. Tribal governments formally list their members, who must meet specific criteria for enrollment. Some require a person to trace half or a quarter of his or her lineage, for instance, to the tribe, while others require only proof of descent.

2 Where did American Indians come from originally?

Many believe that Native peoples originated on this continent, and most tribes have their own creation story. Meanwhile, many anthropologists also have theorized that Indians traveled about 35,000 years ago across a land bridge spanning the Bering Strait from Asia to North America.

3 Why are native peoples referred to as Indians?

Indigenous people in the United States were first referred to as Indians because Columbus believed he had reached the East Indies when he touched the shores of North America. Today, many Native people prefer to call themselves American Indian to avoid stereotypes associated with Indian. "Native American" and "Native" are also acceptable terms and preferred by some. It is always best to refer to Native people by their specific tribe or nation.

4 Which is correct: American Indian or Native American?

Either term is generally acceptable, although individuals may have a preference. Native American gained traction in the 1960s for American Indians and Alaska Natives. Over time, Native American has been expanded to include all native peoples of the continental United States and some in Alaska. (Native American and American Indian are used interchangeably in this guide.)

5 How many American Indians and Natives are there?

There were 2.9 million according to the U.S. Census for 2010, and the number was growing. They represent roughly 1 percent of the overall population. Before Europeans arrived in North America, Native Americans may have numbered as many as 10 million. By the time colonists began keeping records, the population was substantially less, ravaged by war, famine, forced labor and disease from Europeans.

6 Is the number of American Indians declining?

No. The population is young and growing steadily. The American Indian and Alaska Native population increased by 83,250 from July 1, 2006 to July 1, 2007. The U.S. Census projects that the American Indian and Alaska Native population will reach 8.6 million by 2050. That is up from previous forecasts.

7 What are the reasons for rising population?

American Indians and Alaska Natives get better health care and live longer than they did in the recent past. Also, more people are likely to identify themselves as American Indians and Alaska Natives than in earlier Census counts.

8 Why does the government refer to most indigenous people in Alaska as Alaska Natives instead of as American Indians?

Alaska Natives are Eskimo (Inupait and Yupik), Alaskan Indians (Athabascan, Haida, Tlingit and Tsimshian) and Aleut. They are culturally distinct and prefer to be called Alaska Native instead of being grouped as American Indian.

9 Are Native Hawaiians considered American Indians?

No. Native Hawaiians, known as Kanaka Maoli in Hawaiian, trace their lineage and language to Polynesians, including

Tahitians, Maoris and Samoans. Starting in 2000, the federal government recognized Native Hawaiians and Pacific Islanders as a distinct group, including in Census counts. Native Hawaiians often identify with the American Indian push to gain the nation-to-nation relationship that federally recognized tribes have with the United States.

Tribes

10 What is a tribe?

Originally, tribes were societies of people bound by blood ties, family relations and a common language. They also had their own religion and political system. When members of different tribes were forced to live together on reservations, some new tribal groupings formed.

11 How many tribes are there?

In 2014, there were more than 560 federally recognized tribes in the United States, according to the federal Bureau of Indian Affairs, which is required to publish a list every year. This includes more than 225 native villages in Alaska. Federal recognition acknowledges the government-to-government status a tribe has with the United States and provides for certain federal services.

12 OK, there are a lot of different tribes. But aren't American Indians pretty much the same as a group?

No. Indian tribes are as different, for example, as the Irish and Italians. Individual tribes have their own culture, language and tradition. Many groups may be strangers to one another. Some were once enemies.

13 Which is the largest tribe?

Both the Cherokee Nation of Oklahoma and the Navajo Nation estimate tribal membership at 320,000. The Navajo reservation includes parts of Arizona, New Mexico and Utah.

14 Are Indian tribes and Indian nations the same?

Yes. The federally recognized tribes are considered self-governing — or sovereign nations — by Congress. Thus, the federal government deals with them as political entities, not as persons of a particular race. The political status of tribes is written in the U.S. Constitution: "The Congress shall have power . . . to regulate commerce with foreign nations . . . and with the Indian tribes." It is acceptable to refer to American Indians who belong to tribal nations as both tribal members and American citizens, unless an individual has a preference.

15 Can any tribe be federally recognized?

Many tribal nations' federal recognition extends from treaties established in the 18th and 19th centuries. Today, several groups are petitioning for recognition through a rigorous application process. The Bureau of Indian Affairs in the U.S. Department of the Interior maintains a directory of federally recognized tribes. It is at the end of this guide.

16 Can a tribe be recognized by entities other than the U.S. government?

Yes. States can recognize the governmental status of tribes within their borders that the federal government does not. State recognition is often seen as the final step before obtaining federal recognition.

17 What powers do the tribes, as nations, hold?

Federally recognized tribes enjoy the powers of government, except those expressly taken away by Congress or overruled by the Supreme Court. The United States recognizes the tribes' rights to form their own government, determine membership, administer justice, raise taxes, establish businesses and exclude people from reservations. Tribal nations regulate Indian land, resources and the conduct of tribal members on Indian land.

18 What kind of governments do the tribes run?

Most tribal governments are democratic with elected officials in highly developed political systems that often predate European settlers. While similar in structure to American governments, the tribal governments are smaller and have far fewer resources.

19 What is the tribal council?

The tribe's governing body is usually referred to as the tribal council, and is elected by adult members of the tribe. Heading the council is one elected chairperson, president, chief or governor who is the recognized leader. The council performs the legislative aspects of tribal government.

20 Are reservations and tribal governments the same?

No. Tribal governments existed long before reservations were established. However, the governing authority on reservations is the tribal council. In cases where different tribes share a reservation, they often run separate governments, as the Shoshone and Arapaho do in Wyoming.

Reservations

21 What is a reservation?

Indian reservations are areas of land reserved by the federal government as permanent tribal homelands. The United States first established its reservation policy for American Indians in 1787. Today, there are 314 reservations among the last, large tracts of private lands.

22 Why is it called a reservation?

The term originates from the federal government's act of reserving land for federal purposes. In the United States there are two kinds of reserved land that are well known: military and Indian.

23 Do all American Indians live on reservations?

No. More than 60 percent live away from reservations, the U.S. Census reports. However, many return to their tribes' reservations to visit family and attend ceremonies.

24 How much land is held by Native Americans?

About 56 million acres are in reservations and trust land. The Navajo Reservation is the largest, with 16 million acres and occupying parts of Arizona, Utah and New Mexico. Many smaller reservations have less than 1,000 acres.

25 What is trust land?

Land held by the United States for the use and benefit of American Indian tribes. Virtually all trust land is on reservations. Tribes also can purchase land and petition the federal government to hold it in trust, protecting the land from encroachment or seizure. Actions affecting title to trust lands, including sales, are subject to approval of the U.S. Secretary of Interior.

26 Who owns reservations?

The United States holds title to the land for the tribes, with the Department of Interior acting as trustee. The tribe or individual whose land is held in trust is the owner. Non-Indians also own significant portions of reservation land, though tribes may exercise jurisdiction over it.

27 Has the government tried to take away tribal land?

From the 1880s to the 1930s, Congress opened tribal lands to sale, with reservations losing two-thirds of their land base. In the 1950s, the Eisenhower administration adopted a "termination" policy, closing many reservations while trying to assimilate Indians into white society.

28 What kind of mineral reserves do tribal lands have?

Reservations contain a wealth of minerals. The Council of Energy Resource Tribes said that its member tribes own and manage more than 30 percent of the coal west of the Mississippi, 40 percent of domestic uranium and 10 percent of U.S. oil and gas reserves. Other minerals include phosphate, quartz crystal sand, gravel, potash and sodium. Tribes may mine the land or lease mineral rights to others.

29 What is Indian Country?

Indian Country is a legal term used in Title 18 of the U.S. Code. It broadly defines federal and tribal jurisdiction in crimes affecting Indians on reservations. But it also has popular usage, describing reservations and areas with American Indian populations.

30 What are the living conditions in Indian Country?

While health, education and economic conditions have improved in the past several years, Native communities still largely lag behind on most health and economic indicators. Income levels are substantially lower in Indian Country than in the rest of the nation. Indians on reservations are much more likely than the general population to die from accidents, alcoholism, diabetes, pneumonia, suicide, homicide and tuberculosis.

Sovereignty

31 What is tribal sovereignty?

Just like states, tribes have attributes of sovereignty to govern their own territory and internal affairs. The status of tribes as self-governing nations is affirmed and upheld by treaties, case law and the U.S. Constitution. Legal scholars explain that tribes are inherently sovereign, meaning they do not trace their existence to the United States.

32 How does sovereignty work?

The doctrine of tribal sovereignty was affirmed in three Supreme Court rulings in the 1800s. It recognizes the right of American Indian tribes to self-govern and run their internal affairs as "domestic, dependent nations." It keeps states from interfering with that right, while allowing Congress to override an Indian nation's authority.

33 Is sovereignty largely symbolic today?

There is nothing more important to Indian governments and people than sovereignty, tribal leaders say. It is a fundamental principle of the U.S. Constitution. Its legal significance is increasing. Recently, tribes have worked to regain control of their economies and resources by asserting their rights as sovereign powers, sometimes in conflict with neighboring states.

34 What is the government-to-government relationship?

This is federal policy expressing how the United States interacts with tribes. It requires the United States to assess federal actions affecting tribes and to consult with tribes about those actions.

35 How are tribes exercising their status as sovereign nations?

Here are two examples. The Isleta Pueblo tribe required the city of Albuquerque, N.M., to abide by its clean-water standards, which are stricter and costlier than state requirements. In the Pacific Northwest, tribes partner with state and federal governments to co-manage fisheries and protect salmon stock.

36 What is sovereign immunity?

It is the ability of a government to define the terms upon which it can be sued. Tribes have invoked sovereign immunity in suits that challenge their authority to regulate land use. There have been recent efforts in Congress to limit a tribe's sovereign immunity, but they have not been adopted.

37 Do states have jurisdiction over American Indians or their land?

States do not have any civil or criminal jurisdiction in Indian Country unless Congress delegates it or the federal courts determine it exists. The 1988 Indian Gaming Regulatory Act, adopted by Congress, requires tribes and states to enter into compacts, or agreements, before gambling operations can open on Indian land.

38 Do American Indians have to obey the same laws as non-Indians?

When tribal members are off reservations, they are generally subject to local, state and federal laws. On reservations, they are subject only to federal and tribal laws. Under federal law known as the Assimilative Crimes Act, any violation of state criminal law on reservations is a federal crime.

39 Are American Indians U.S. citizens?

Yes. Indians have dual citizenship as tribal members and as American citizens. Congress extended citizenship to American Indians in 1924.

40 Can American Indians vote?

American Indians and Alaska Natives have the same right to vote as other American citizens. They vote in local, state, federal and tribal elections. Each tribe determines voting criteria for tribal elections.

41 Do Native Americans pay state or federal taxes?

They pay the same taxes as everyone else with the following exceptions: Native Americans employed on reservations do not pay state income taxes. American Indians living on trust land are free from local and state property taxes. Generally, state sales taxes are not levied on Indian transactions made on reservations. Indians do not pay federal income taxes on money earned from trust lands, such as fees received for grazing rights and oil drilling.

Treaties

42 What are treaties?

From 1777 to 1871, U.S. relations with Indian nations were negotiated through legally binding agreements called treaties. These treaties, or agreements, between tribal governments and the United States transferred and created property rights as well as service obligations. There were 371 treaties signed with American Indian tribes, usually to gain rights to their land.

43 What agreements did the treaties contain?

The treaties often promised Indians protection, goods, services, self-governing rights, health care and a tribal homeland in exchange for cooperation and vast tracts of land.

44 Why did European settlers enter into treaties with the tribes?

Tribes had power because of their military strength and knowledge of the land. They could have forced Europeans off the continent, if they had banded together. European law also taught colonists that land transactions required legal documentation.

45 Why did the tribes agree to the treaties?

Faced with giving up their lands or losing their people to war, disease and a rising tide of settlers, tribes entered into the agreements. The tribes view treaties as solemn moral obligations.

46 Were treaties broken?

Throughout the years, conflicting federal policy and court rulings resulted in Native peoples losing some of their civil rights and lands. An early example was the Trail of Tears, the forced march of 14,000 Cherokees from Georgia, Alabama and Tennessee to Oklahoma, despite a 1791 treaty granting them a permanent homeland in the East. About 4,000 Cherokees — mostly babies, children and old people — died from starvation, exposure and disease.

47 Are Native Americans affected by the Affordable Care Act?

Yes. There have been broad changes since tribes entered agreements that guaranteed rights to services like health care. Native Americans who live in areas not served by the Indian Health Service or who don't have insurance through work can get covered under the Affordable Care Act. However, they are not subject to the individual mandate. In other words, there's no penalty if Native Americans remain uninsured.

48 What is trust responsibility?

The federal Indian trust responsibility is considered one of the more important principles in federal Indian law. It is a legally enforceable fiduciary obligation of the United States to protect tribal lands, assets, resources and treaty rights. Supreme Court rulings suggest that trust responsibility entails legal as well as moral duties.

49 What happens if the federal government fails to uphold its trust responsibilities?

The federal government's mismanagement of Indian trust accounts dating back to the 1880s was the subject of a $3.4 billion class-action lawsuit settled in 2011. It was the largest class-action settlement for the federal government in U.S. history. The case's lead plaintiff was Elouise Cobell, a member of the Blackfeet tribe. She contended the government mismanaged nearly $150 billion in royalties owed to Indian landowners. Part of the final settlement has been paid out to Indian landowners. Large portions of money were being used for Indian education and a land buy-back program.

50 Are treaties still valid?

Although the government stopped entering into treaties with Indian tribes in 1871, the Constitution holds treaties as "the supreme law of the land." Once signed, a treaty stays in effect unless superseded by acts of Congress or other treaties.

51 Do treaties grant Native Americans special rights today?

In the Pacific Northwest, tribes are able to hunt, fish and gather food as their ancestors did. On all reservations, tribes have access to education and medical care provided by the federal government under treaty obligations. These are examples of Indian rights based on treaties signed years ago.

52 Are treaties being challenged?

There are many efforts in modern times to dilute and challenge treaty rights. Bills have been introduced in Congress to limit tribal self-governance and to give states authority over tribes. No major changes have been enacted, however.

53 Is there an organization that represents tribal interests?

There are many. The largest is the National Congress of American Indians. It was founded on principles that include protecting tribal sovereignty and rights. The Native American Rights Fund champions issues of sovereignty, human rights and government accountability that go before the nation's courts. The Native American Journalists Association evaluates and supports free press efforts in Indian Country as well as the fair and accurate representation of Native Americans in the news media. The American Indian Movement, an activist group, was founded in 1968 to promote civil rights for Native Americans through sit-ins and highly visible protests. AIM is still active.

Federal Offices

54 What does the Bureau of Indians Affairs do?

The bureau is the principal federal agency working with tribes. Its job is to provide services and funds that benefit tribal members. Unlike the 1800s, when the bureau was in the War Department, the bureau's stated goal is to help tribes with self-determination. Almost 100 percent of its employees are tribal members.

55 How does someone qualify for BIA services?

Persons must belong to a federally recognized tribe.

56 What services does the BIA provide?

The bureau funds law enforcement, social services, land management, forestry services, education and more.

57 What other federal offices work with tribes?

Just about all federal agencies work with Indian tribes. The Health and Human Services Department, for example, runs the Indian Health Services, which provides medical care on or near reservations. The Justice Department has the Office of Tribal Justice, which coordinates much of the law enforcement effort in Indian Country.

58 Do American Indians have the right to hold elective office?

Indians have the same rights as all U.S. citizens, and have held almost all levels of elective office. Charles Curtis, a member of the Kaw tribe, was vice president under Herbert Hoover. Ben Nighthorse Campbell, a Republican U.S. senator from Colorado until 2005, is a member of the Northern Cheyenne tribe. Campbell also served three terms in the U.S. House of Representatives as a Democrat.

59 Do Native Americans serve in the U.S. armed forces?

Native Americans have fought in all American wars since the Revolution. One out of four Indian men is a U.S. military veteran. Native Americans' patriotism in World War I led Congress to pass the Indian Citizenship Act of 1924. In World War II, Navajo Marines used their language as a code to transmit messages that enemies of the United States failed to break.

Casinos

60 Who regulates Indian casinos?

The National Indian Gaming Commission, established by Congress, oversees bingo operations, casinos and certain other types of gambling on tribal land. It sets rules for licensing, reviews yearly audits, and approves ordinances that tribes develop to run gaming operations. The U.S. Departments of Treasury, Justice and Interior have authority over aspects of Indian gaming. Indian nations, as well, have their own gaming commissions, tribal police forces and court systems.

61 What is the Indian Gaming Regulatory Act?

This federal law requires states to enter into compacts with tribal governments that plan to engage in casino gambling, including slot machines and blackjack. Gaming must be conducted on tribal land, and the states' control is limited to the terms in the compacts. The U.S. Secretary of the Interior must approve the compacts.

62 How much money do Indian gaming operators make each year?

In 2012, they reported a total of $27.9 billion in revenues. Not all tribes get rich, though. A few large gaming tribes earn most of that revenue. The more successful operations are usually located in or near large metropolitan areas.

63 Is Indian gaming a major player in the gambling industry?

Indian gaming is growing rapidly, but represents only 8 percent of the revenue market share, according to the National Indian Gaming Association.

64 Do all tribes have casino gambling?

No. The National Indian Gaming Association counted 420 gaming establishments, associated with nearly 240 tribes across 28 states. That is fewer than half of all tribes. Most operations are considered to be small to moderate and many are limited to bingo.

65 Do the tribes pay taxes on their revenues?

No. As sovereign governments, they do not pay taxes on their revenues to state or federal governments. However, states can assess fees on the tribes for costs of gambling regulation and administration. Some states, including Michigan, Connecticut and Washington, have formal arrangements with tribes to receive additional revenue. Casino workers are generally subject to the same payroll and income taxes other Americans pay.

66 Are individual tribes getting rich from casinos?

While gaming has helped tribes such as the Grand Traverse Band of Ottawa and Chippewa in Michigan stem poverty, Indians are the nation's poorest population. They rank at the bottom of almost every social and economic measure.

67 How do tribes use gaming revenue?

The Indian Gaming Regulatory Act requires tribal governments to spend revenue on operations, welfare, economic development and charity. Tribes that meet those obligations can seek U.S. Secretary of the Interior permission for per-capita distribution plans to benefit members. Forty-seven tribes have approval to do so.

68 Why are Indian casinos a popular enterprise among the tribes?

Gambling is an accepted tradition that figured in celebrations and ceremonies long before European settlement. With many reservations in distant and remote areas, gaming is one of the few viable sources of employment and revenue.

69 Do all American Indians favor gambling?

No. Some argue that the gambling operations hurt their culture, and that tribes with casinos show less interest in traditional ways and religious functions.

Education

70 What is a tribal school?

Since the early 1800s, the Bureau of Indian Affairs assumed responsibility for the education of children on reservations through Indian schools. In 1978, the federal government began turning over school control to the tribes, while still providing oversight and funding. The bureau funds or operates 187 schools and serves 50,000 students.

71 How many American Indian students attend public schools off the reservation?

About 480,000 American Indian children attend public schools off reservations. Some states with large populations of Indian schoolchildren provide funds for Indian language and cultural education.

72 What proportion of American Indians are college graduates?

In 2010, 76 percent of American Indians who were at least 25 years old were high school graduates, according to the U.S. Census. Thirteen percent had at least a bachelor's degree.

73 What is a tribal college?

There are more than 30 fully accredited tribal colleges in the United States, according to the American Indian College Fund. The schools were individually established to meet the needs of students on reservations, often located in remote areas underserved by other post-secondary institutions. Most are two-year schools that focus on local economic development and work-force training.

74 How are tribal colleges funded?

The 1981 Tribally Controlled Community College Assistance Act provides operational funds for 25 tribal colleges. All the colleges receive support from the U.S. Department of Agriculture as land-grant institutions, and from the U.S. Department of Education. In addition, they may receive competitive grants, foundation money and private support. But the colleges receive little or no state funds, and are not supported through property taxes, as are many mainstream community colleges.

75 Do Native Americans get a free college education?

While some tribes offer stipends or scholarships to members, Native Americans as a group do not receive free college educations. Some public university systems, like the state of Montana's, and specific colleges have arranged to waive tuition for Native American students who meet a set of criteria. This is rare. Many students qualify for federal help and other needs-based aid because they meet poverty guidelines for all students. Eighty-five percent of students at tribal colleges live in poverty.

76 How do graduation rates for American Indians compare with the general population?

College graduation rates are lower for American Indians than for any other minority group, according to the American Indian Higher Education Consortium. Only 30 percent of American Indian students completed a bachelor's degree within six years of enrolling, compared with 54 percent of all students.

Language

77 Do American Indians speak their own language?

The vast majority of Indians speak English as their main language, though some know their Native language as well. When Europeans first arrived here, about 350 Indian languages were spoken.

78 How many American Indian languages are still spoken?

The precise number is unknown. It is estimated that about 200 languages are spoken. Native American languages are classified geographically rather than linguistically, since they do not belong to a single linguistic family, as Indo-European languages do.

79 Which are the most common languages?

There is no standard American Indian language. A number are spoken regularly by larger tribes, such as Navajo (spoken by 80,000) and Ojibwe (spoken by 40,000).

80 Were there written Indian languages?

Before European settlement in North America, Indian writing was in pictographs, such as the birch-bark scrolls inscribed by the Ojibwe. Exposure to written European languages, including their direct study, resulted in several groups developing their own forms of writing.

81 Are American Indian languages continuing to die out?

Yes. More than a third are spoken only by elders and may not survive to the next generation, according to "The Handbook of North American Indians: Language." Some languages are known to just two or three speakers.

82 What is being done to preserve American Indian languages?

Tribes have written language books and have created teaching tools for Indian schools. Some languages are taught in universities. In cases where the number of speakers has dwindled, language might ultimately die out.

Religion

83 Is there an American Indian religion?

There are many Native American traditions and beliefs among the more than 500 tribes. In many tribes, beliefs are an integral part of daily life and are not considered part of a religion reliant on an institution for worship. Prayers have taken a variety of forms, including songs and dances and acts such as sprinkling tobacco or corn meal. In the 19th century, Native Americans lost many of their religious customs as colonists forced them to convert to Christianity. Colonists sent Native children to mission schools and banned some Indian ceremonies.

84 How many American Indians identify themselves as Christians?

In the 1990s, more than two-thirds of Native Americans identified themselves at least nominally as Christians. Others combine Christian beliefs with their native religions or practice separate faiths.

85 Are Native Americans free to practice their native religion?

Until the 1930s the United States tried to ban Native American religious rituals, including the Ghost Dance, Sun Dance and peyote prayer meetings. In 1978, Congress passed the American Indian Religious Freedom Act, an official expression of goodwill toward Native American spirituality. Many religious practices once considered on the verge of disappearing were revived. These include pipe ceremonials, sweat lodges, vision quests and Sun Dances.

86 What is a sweat lodge?

Much like a sauna, sweat lodges are heated by fire or by pouring water over hot stones. Some Native Americans use the lodges to induce sweating for medicinal and spiritual purposes.

87 What is a vision quest?

In some traditional Native religions, Indians practice meditation and fasting to receive a vision to guide them in their lives. Often, one separates from the tribe and enters the wilderness to seek a vision or guardian spirit.

88 How does tobacco figure in American Indian religion?

Tobacco has been regarded as the most sacred plant, used in Indian religion, medicine and diplomacy. Smoking at gatherings was a symbol of hospitality. Sharing a pipe sealed treaties, and sprinkling leaves ensured a good harvest. Ritualistic use of tobacco continues today.

89 Did Native Americans learn about tobacco from white settlers?

On the contrary. Native peoples introduced tobacco and the pipe to white explorers. Native Americans had been smoking tobacco for a thousand years or more by the time Columbus returned to Spain with some leaves, and its use spread across Europe.

Culture

90 What is cultural misappropriation?

This is when people claim an ancestry or culture that is not their own. At its heart, it means someone is not being authentic or is taking something that does not belong to them. Such accusations arose when Johnny Depp played Tonto in "The Lone Ranger." Some also questioned the claim of Indian ancestry by Elizabeth Warren, a Democratic candidate for the U.S. Senate. This term can also mean using cultural or sacred symbols on costumes or decoration. Cultural appropriation can happen with any group.

91 Why do Native Americans object to the use of Indian symbols, like feathers and face paint, in U.S. sports?

Many Native Americans believe the use of Indian symbols by sports teams and fans trivializes their way of life. For example, some Native Americans take offense when fans paint their faces at football games. In traditional Native cultures, face-painting is reserved for sacred ceremonies, some of which include weddings and funerals.

92 Why do American Indians object to the term "redskin" used by the Washington NFL franchise?

The word is an overtly racist term that can be compared to the N-word. Using tribal names and Native American images as team names or mascots is also an issue. Indian mascots can trivialize Native heritage, perpetuate stereotypes or encourage mocking cheers and behaviors. The NFL name goes beyond that, given its overtly racist history. Some media outlets have stopped using the name. The Native American Journalists Association supports that.

93 What is a peace pipe?

When various tribes dominated North America, carrying a pipe signified peaceful intent, a passport universally honored, according to "A Guide to America's Indians." White explorers carried "peace pipes" for chance meetings with Indians.

94 Why is an eagle feather significant to American Indians?

Certain symbols, including the eagle feather, seem to be universal in their importance to the various tribes. The eagle is revered for its strength, size and intelligence. Its feathers are used in religious ceremonies.

95 How do American Indians obtain the feathers of a protected bird like the eagle?

The U.S. Fish and Wildlife Service administers a program that makes the feathers available to Indian religious practitioners. The feathers are from eagles that die naturally or by accident.

96 What is a medicine bundle?

It is a collection of objects believed to heal disease and ward off enemies. Traditionally, individuals, households and villages kept medicine bundles for self-protection. The bundles might contain herbs, stone, pollen, horns, bone, teeth and feathers.

97 What is a powwow?

Powwow comes from the Narragansett word for shaman. It is a celebration and social gathering, honoring sacred Indian traditions through dancing, drumming, singing and the gathering of people. Powwows may be held to honor an individual or for a special occasion. Most commonly, the powwow is a social event.

98 Are non-Natives welcome at powwows?

There are ceremonial powwows that are closed to non-tribal members, but everyone is welcome at a publicized powwow.

99 What are teepees?

The teepee, or tipi, is a dwelling used by nomadic Plains tribes. Made from buffalo hides, it was stretched over a cone formed by poles, which made it strong and easy to move. Similar to the teepee, the wickiup was used by tribes to the south. It was made from brush secured over arched poles. The wigwam of the eastern woodlands was a domed or conical frame covered with bark or mats. These traditional dwellings are no longer used as everyday, year-round shelters.

100 How can a person trace his or her Indian ancestry?

The first step is basic genealogical research to obtain specific information on ancestors' names, birth dates, marriages and deaths, and places where they lived. The next step is to find out if ancestors are on official tribal rolls. For information, write to the National Archives and Records Administration, Natural Resources Branch, Civil Archives Division, 8th and Pennsylvania Ave., NW, Washington, D.C. 20408. After determining tribal heritage, individuals should contact individual tribes to learn about membership. Tribes have the final determination on who qualifies.

566 Federally Recognized Tribes

Source: USA.gov, the federal government's official web portal.

- Absentee Shawnee Tribe, OK
- Accohannock Indian Tribe, MD
- Afognak Native Village, AK
- Agua Caliente Band of Cahuilla Indians, CA
- Ak-Chin Indian Community of the Maricopa, AZ
- Alaska Tribes and Villages
- Aroostook Band of Micmacs, ME
- Bad River Band of Lake Superior Chippewa Tribe, WI
- Barona Band of Mission Indians, CA
- Bay Mills Indian Community, MI
- Big Sandy Rancheria, CA
- Big Valley Band of Pomo Indians, CA
- Blackfeet Nation, MT
- Brothertown Indian Nation, WI
- Buena Vista Rancheria of Me-Wuk Indians, CA
- Burns Paiute Tribe, OR
- Cabazon Band of Mission Indians, CA
- Cahto Indian Tribe of the Laytonville Rancheria, CA
- California Valley Miwok Tribe, CA
- Camp Kumeyaay Nation, CA
- Catawba Indian Nation, SC
- Cedarville Rancheria, CA

- Chehalis Confederated Tribes, WA
- Chemehuevi Indian Tribe, CA
- Cher Ae Heights Indian Community of the Trinidad Rancheria, CA
- Cherokee Nation, OK
- Cherokee Tribe, AL
- Cheyenne-Arapaho Tribes, OK
- Chickaloon Village Traditional Council, AK
- Chickasaw Nation, OK
- Chignik Bay Tribal Council, AK
- Chilkat Indian Village (Klukwan), AK
- Chitimacha Tribe, LA
- Choctaw Nation, FL
- Choctaw Nation, OK
- Citizen Potawatomi Nation, OK
- Cloverdale Rancheria of Pomo Indians, CA
- Cocopah Indian Tribe, AZ
- Coeur D´Alene Tribe, ID
- Colorado River Indian Tribes, AZ and CA
- Comanche Nation, OK
- Confederated Tribes of the Colville Reservation, WA
- Coos, Lower Umpqua and Siuslaw Indians Confederated Tribes, OR
- Coquille Indian Tribe, OR
- Costanoan Rumsen Carmel Tribe, CA
- Cowasuck Band of the Pennacook - Abenaki, MA
- Cow Creek Band of Umpqua Tribe of Indians, OR
- Cowlitz Indian Tribe, WA
- Crow Creek Sioux Tribe, SD
- Crow Tribe Apsáalooke Nation, MT
- Curyung Tribal Council, AK

- Delaware Nation, OK
- Dry Creek Rancheria Band of Pomo Indians, CA
- Eastern Band of the Cherokee Nation, NC
- Eastern Chickahominy Tribe, VA
- Eastern Shoshone Tribe of the Wind River Reservation, WY
- Echota Cherokee Tribe, AL
- Eklutna Native Village, AK
- Elem Indian Colony, CA
- Elk Valley Rancheria, CA
- Enterprise Rancheria of Maidu Indians, CA
- Eyak Native Village, AK
- Fallon Paiute-Shoshone Tribe, NV
- Federated Indians of Graton Rancheria, CA
- Flandreau Santee Sioux Tribe, SD
- Forest County Potawatomi, WI
- Fort Belknap Indian Nations, MT
- Fort McDowell Yavapai Nation, AZ
- Fort Mojave Indian Tribe, AZ
- Fort Peck Assiniboine and Sioux Tribes, MT
- Fort Yukon Native Village, AK
- Georgetown Tribal Council (Georgetown Native Village), AK
- Gila River Indian Community, AZ
- Grand Traverse Band of Ottawa and Chippewa Indians, MI
- Greenville Rancheria, CA
- Gulkana Village, AK
- Habematolel Pomo of Upper Lake, CA
- Hannahville Indian Community, MI
- Havasupai Tribe of the Havasupai Reservation, AZ

- Ho-Chunk Nation, WI
- Hoh Indian Tribe, WA
- Hoopa Valley Tribe, CA
- Hopi Tribe, AZ
- Hopland Band of Pomo Indians, CA
- Houlton Band of Maliseet Indians, ME
- Hualapai Indian Tribe, AZ
- Iliamna Village Council, AK
- Ione Band of Miwok Indians, CA
- Iowa Nation, OK
- Iowa Tribe, KS & NE
- Jamestown S´Klallam Tribe, WA
- Jamul Indian Village, CA
- Jatibonicu Taino Tribal Band, NJ
- Jatibonicu Taino Tribal Nation of Boriken, PR
- Jena Band of Choctaw Indians, LA
- Jicarilla Apache Nation, NM
- Kaibab Band of Paiute Indians, AZ
- Kake Organized Village, AK
- Kalispel Tribe of Indians, WA
- Karuk Tribe, CA
- Kashaya Band of Pomo Indians, CA
- Kashia Band of Pomo Indians of the Stewarts Point Rancheria, CA
- Kaw Nation, OK
- Kenaitze Indian Tribe, AK
- Ketchikan Indian Corporation, AK
- Keweenaw Bay Indian Community, MI
- Kickapoo Tribe, KS
- King Island Native Community, AK
- Klamath Tribes, OR

- Knik Tribe, AK
- Koasek (Cowasuck) Traditional Band Council of the Sovereign Abenaki Nation, VT
- Kootenai Tribe, ID
- Kotzebue Native Village, AK
- Kumeyaay Nation, CA
- Lac Courte Oreilles Band of Ojibwe, WI
- Lac du Flambeau Band of Lake Superior Chippewa Indians, WI
- Lac Vieux Desert Band of Lake Superior Chippewa Indians, MI
- La Jolla Band of Luiseno Mission Indians, CA
- Little River Band of Ottawa Indians, MI
- Little Traverse Bay Bands of Odawa Indians, MI
- Lower Brule Sioux Tribe of the Lower Brule Reservation, SD
- Lower Elwha Tribal Community, WA
- Lumbee Tribe, NC
- Lummi Nation, WA
- Makah Indian Tribe, WA
- Mandan, Hidatsa, and Arikara Nation, ND
- Mashantucket Pequot, CT
- Mashpee Wampanoag Tribe, MA
- Match-e-be-nash-she-wish Band of Pottawatomi, MI
- Mechoopda Maidu Indians, CA
- Mendota Mdewakanton Dakota Community, MN
- Menominee Indian Tribe, WI
- Mescalero Apache Tribe, NM
- Me-Wuk Indians of the Buena Vista Rancheria, CA
- Miami Nation, OK
- Miccosukee Seminole Nation, FL

- Miccosukee Tribe of Indians, FL
- Mille Lacs Band of Ojibwe, MN
- Minnesota Chippewa Tribe, MN
- Mission Indians – Barona Band, CA
- Mission Indians – Cabazon Band, CA
- Mississippi Band of Choctaw Indians, MS
- Miwok Tribe - California Valley, CA
- Mohegan Tribe, CT
- Mohican Nation, WI
- Monacan Indian Nation, VA
- Morongo Band of Cahuilla Mission Indians, CA
- Muckleshoot Tribe, WA
- Muscogee (Creek) Nation, OK
- Nansemond Indian Tribal Association, VA
- Napaimute Native Village, AK
- Narragansett Indian Tribe, RI
- Navajo Nation, AZ
- Nez Perce Tribe, ID
- Ninilchik Village Tribe, AK
- Nisqually Indian Tribe, WA
- Nome Eskimo Community, AK
- Nooksack Indian Tribe, WA
- Northern Arapaho Tribe, WY
- Northern Cheyenne Tribe, MT
- North Fork Rancheria of Mono Indians, CA
- Northwestern Band of the Shoshone Nation, UT
- Oglala Sioux Tribe, SD
- Oneida Nation, WI
- Onondaga Nation, NY
- Osage Tribe, OK
- Ottawa Tribe, OK

- Pala Band of Mission Indians, CA
- Pascua Yaqui Tribe, AZ
- Pawnee Nation, OK
- Pechanga Band of Luiseno Indians, CA
- Penobscot Indian Nation, ME
- Peoria Tribe, OK
- Picayune Rancheria of Chukchansi Indians, CA
- Pinoleville Pomo Nation, CA
- Poarch Band of Creek Indians, AL
- Pokagon Band of Potawatomi Indians, MI & IN
- Pomo Indians of the Cloverdale Rancheria, CA
- Ponca Tribe, NE
- Ponca Tribe of Indians, OK
- Port Gamble S'Klallam Tribe, WA
- Port Lions Native Village, AK
- Powhatan Renape Nation, NJ
- Prairie Band of Potawatomi, KS
- Prairie Island Indian Community, MN
- Pueblo of Cochiti, NM
- Pueblo of Isleta, NM
- Pueblo of Jemez, NM
- Pueblo of Laguna, NM
- Pueblo of Sandia, NM
- Pueblo of Santa Ana, NM
- Pueblo of Taos, NM
- Pueblo of Zuni, NM
- Puyallup Tribe, WA
- Pyramid Lake Paiute Tribes, NV
- Qawalangin Tribe of Unalaska, AK
- Quapaw Tribe of Indians, OK
- Quileute Tribe, WA

- Quinault Indian Nation, WA
- Red Cliff Band of Lake Superior Chippewa, WI
- Redding Rancheria, CA
- Red Lake Nation, MN
- Rincon Band of Luiseno Mission Indians, CA
- Robinson Rancheria of Pomo Indians, CA
- Rosebud Sioux Tribe, SD
- Round Valley Indian Tribes, CA
- Rumsey Indian Rancheria of Wintun Indians, CA
- Sac & Fox Nation, OK
- Sac & Fox Tribe of the Mississippi (Meskwaki), IA
- Saginaw Chippewa Indian Tribe, MI
- Salish & Kootenai Confederated Tribes, MT
- Salt River Pima-Maricopa Indian Community, AZ
- Samish Indian Nation, WA
- San Carlos Apache Tribe, AZ
- San Carlos Apache Tribe, AZ
- San Manuel Band, CA
- San Manuel Band of Serrano Mission Indians, CA
- Santa Ynez Band of Chumash Mission Indians, CA
- Santee Sioux Nation, NE
- Sauk-Suiattle Indian Tribe, WA
- Sault Ste. Marie Tribe of Chippewa Indians, MI
- Seldovia Village Tribe, AK
- Seminole Nation, OK
- Seminole Tribe, FL
- Seneca-Cayuga Tribe, OK
- Seneca Nation of Indians, NY
- Shakopee Mdewakanton Sioux Community, MN
- Shawnee Tribe, OK
- Shingle Springs Band of Miwok Indians, CA

- Shoalwater Bay Indian Tribe, WA
- Shoshone-Bannock Tribes, ID
- Shoshone-Paiute Tribes, NV
- Siletz Indians Confederated Tribes, OR
- Sisseton-Wahpeton Oyate, SD
- Sitka Tribe, AK
- Skokomish Tribal Nation, WA
- Smith River Rancheria, CA
- Snoqualmie Tribe, WA
- Soboba Band of Luiseno Indians, CA
- Sokaogon Chippewa Community, WI
- Southern Cherokee Nation, KY
- Southern Cherokee Nation, OK
- Southern Ute Indian Tribe, CO
- Spirit Lake Tribe, ND
- Spokane Tribe, WA
- Squaxin Island Tribe, WA
- St. Regis Mohawk Tribe, NY
- Standing Rock Sioux Tribe, ND & SD
- Stebbins Community Association, AK
- Stillaguamish Tribe, WA
- Stockbridge Munsee Community, WI
- Summit Lake Paiute Tribe, NV
- Sun'aq Tribe of Kodiak, AK
- Suquamish Tribe, WA
- Susanville Indian Rancheria, CA
- Swinomish Indian Tribe, WA
- Sycuan Band of the Kumeyaay Nation, CA
- Tachi Yokut Tribe, CA
- Te-Moak Tribe of Western Shoshone, NV
- Timbisha Shoshone Tribe, CA and NV

- Tlingit and Haida Indian Tribes, AK
- Tohono O'odham Nation, AZ
- Tonkawa Tribe, OK
- Tulalip Tribes, WA
- Tule River Tribe, CA
- Tunica-Biloxi Tribe, LA
- Turtle Mountain Band of Chippewa Indians, ND
- Ugashik Traditional Council, AK
- Umatilla Indian Reservation Confederated Tribes, OR
- Unalakleet Native Village, AK
- United Auburn Indian Community, CA
- United Keetoowah Band of Cherokee Indians, OK
- Upper Sioux Community, MN
- Ute Indian Tribe, UT
- Ute Mountain Tribe, CO, NM, & UT
- Viejas Band of Kumeyaay Indians, CA
- Wales Native Village, AK
- Walker River Paiute Tribe, NV
- Wampanoag Tribe of Gay Head, MA
- Warm Springs Reservation Confederated Tribes, OR
- Washoe Tribe, NV & CA
- White Mountain Apache Tribe, AZ
- Winnebago Tribe, NE
- Wiyot Tribe, CA
- Woody Island Tribal Council, AK
- Wyandotte Nation, OK
- Yakama Nation Confederated Tribes and Bands, WA
- Yakutat Tlingit Tribe, AK
- Yankton Sioux Tribe, SD
- Yavapai-Apache Nation, AZ
- Yavapai-Prescott Tribe, AZ

- Ysleta Del Sur Pueblo, TX
- Yurok Tribe, CA

Organizations and Agencies

- American Indian College Fund: http://www.collegefund.org/
- American Indian Higher Education Consortium: http://aihec.org/
- American Indian Movement: http://www.aimovement.org/
- American Indian Science and Engineering Society: http://www.aises.org/
- Association on American Indian Affairs: http://www.indian-affairs.org
- Association of Tribal Archives, Libraries and Museums: http://www.atalm.org/
- Bureau of Indian Affairs: http://www.bia.gov/
- Indian Health Service: http://www.ihs.gov/
- Labriola National American Indian Data Center: https://lib.asu.edu/labriola
- National Congress of American Indians: http://www.ncai.org/
- National Indian Child Welfare Association: http://www.nicwa.org/
- National Indian Education Association: http://www.niea.org/
- National Indian Gaming Association: http://www.indiangaming.org/
- National Museum of the American Indian: http://www.nmai.si.edu/home/

- Native American Journalists Association: http://www.naja.com/
- The Native American Rights Fund: http://www.narf.org/
- Native Ways Federation: htttp://nativewaysfederation.org/
- Newberry Consortium in American Indian Studies: http://www.newberry.org/newberry-consortium-american-indian-studies
- Office of the Special Trustee for American Indians: http://www.doi.gov/ost/index.cfm
- Running String for American Indian Youth: http://indianyouth.org/
- U.S. Census Bureau: http://www.census.gov/newsroom/releases/archives/facts_for_features_special_editions/cb13-ff26.html

Also in This Series

100 Questions and Answers About Indian Americans
100 Questions and Answers About Americans
100 Questions and Answers About Arab Americans
100 Questions and Answers About Hispanics and Latinos
100 Questions and Answers About East Asian Cultures

For copies

Copies of this guide in paperback or ebook formats may be ordered from Amazon.

For a volume discount on copies or a special edition customized and branded for your university or organization, contact David Crumm Media, LLC at info@DavidCrummMedia.com.

For more information and further discussion visit: news.jrn.msu.edu/culturalcompetence

Resources

- Deloria Jr., Vine and Clifford Lytle. *The Nations Within: The Past and Future of American Indian Sovereignty*. Austin: University of Texas Press, 1998.
- Marquis, Arnold. *A Guide to America's Indians*. Norman: University of Oklahoma Press, 1974.
- Reed, James B. and Judy A. Zelio. *States and Tribes Building New Traditions*. Washington, D.C.: National Conference of State Legislatures, 1995.
- Robbins, Catherine C. *All Indians Do Not Live in Teepees (or Casinos)*. Lincoln: University of Nebraska Press' Bison Books, 2011.
- Smith, Paul Chaat. *Everything You Know about Indians Is Wrong*. Minneapolis: University of Minnesota Press (Indigenous Americas Series), 2009.
- Tallbear, Kim. *Native American DNA: Tribal Belonging and the False Promise of Genetic Science*. Minneapolis: University of Minnesota Press, 2013.
- Treuer, Anton. *Everything You Wanted to Know about Indians but Were Afraid to Ask*. Nepean: Borealis Books, 2012.

If you enjoyed this book, you may also enjoy

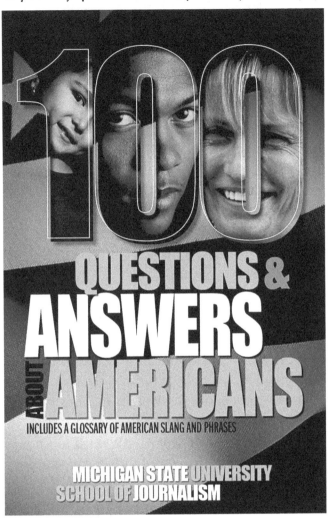

This questions and answers guide from the Michigan
State University School of Journalism provides 100
answers to basic questions about Americans.

http://news.jrn.msu.edu/culturalcompetence/

ISBN: 978-1-939880-20-8

If you enjoyed this book, you may also enjoy

This questions and answers guide from the Michigan
State University School of Journalism provides 100
answers to basic questions about East Asian cultures.

http://news.jrn.msu.edu/culturalcompetence/

ISBN: 978-939880-50-5

If you enjoyed this book, you may also enjoy

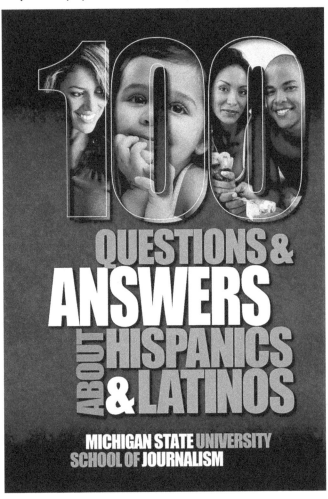

This questions and answers guide from the Michigan
State University School of Journalism provides 100
answers to basic questions about Hispanics and Latinos

http://news.jrn.msu.edu/culturalcompetence/

ISBN: 978-1-939880-44-4

If you enjoyed this book, you may also enjoy

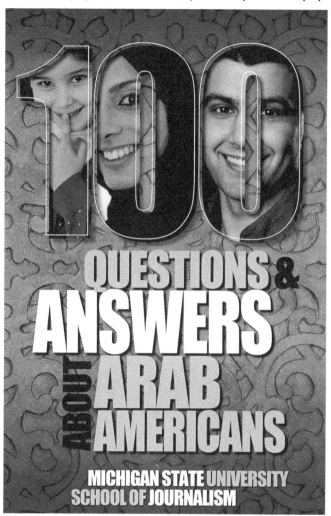

This questions and answers guide from the Michigan
State University School of Journalism provides 100
answers to basic questions about Arab Americans.

http://news.jrn.msu.edu/culturalcompetence/

978-1-939880-56-7

CPSIA information can be obtained
at www.ICGtesting.com
Printed in the USA
LVHW101627090522
718280LV00015B/227